Weather Watch

written by Jacquie Kilkenny

CW00866898

Engage Literacy is published in 2013 by Raintree.
Raintree is an imprint of Capstone Global Library Limited, a company incorporated in Engand and Wales having its registered office at 7 Pilgrim Street, London, EC4V 6LB – Registered company number: 6695582
www.raintreepublishers.co.uk

Originally published in Australia by Hinkler Education, a division of Hinkler Books Pty Ltd.
Text and illustration copyright © Hinkler Books Pty Ltd 2012

Written by Jacquie Kilkenny
Lead authors Jay Dale and Anne Giulieri
Illustrations on pp 6–7, 14 by Cherie Zamazing; pp 12, 24 by Gaston Vanzet
Edited by Gwenda Smyth
UK edition edited by Dan Nunn, Catherine Veitch and Sian Smith
Designed by Susannah Low, Butterflyrocket Design

All rights reserved. No part of this publication may be reproduced, stored in a retrieval system, or transmitted in any way or by any means, electronic, mechanical, photocopying, recording or otherwise, without the prior written permission of Capstone Global Library Limited.

Weather Watch
ISBN: 978 1 406 26505 7
10 9 8 7 6 5 4 3 2 1

Printed and bound in China by Leo Paper Products Ltd

Acknowledgements

Cover images (left to right): © Emilia Ungur | Dreamstime.com; © Adam Gryko | Dreamstime.com; © Aleksandr Stikhin | Dreamstime.com; p4 top: © Gunold Brunbauer | Dreamstime.com; p4 bottom: iStockphoto.com/ © Troels Graugaard; p5 top: © Winzworks | Dreamstime.com; p5 bottom: © Marcin Pawinski | Dreamstime.com; p6: © Rozenn Leard | Dreamstime.com; p7(main): iStockphoto.com/ © Crisma; p7(inset): iStockphoto.com/ © Rivetti; p8 top left (and back cover): © Tina Rencelj | Dreamstime.com; p8 top right: © Melinda Fawver | Dreamstime.com; p8 bottom right (and title page): © Aleksandr Stikhin | Dreamstime.com; p8 background: © Adam Gryko | Dreamstime.com; p9 top left: iStockphoto.com/ © Karen Massier; p9 top right: © Clearviewstock | Dreamstime.com; p9 bottom: © Vladyslav Siaber | Dreamstime.com; p9 background: © Mitar Gavric | Dreamstime.com; p10 bottom left: © Goodluz | Dreamstime.com; p10 bottom right: Gallo Images/SuperStock; p10 inset: © Sofiaworld | Dreamstime.com; p11 top left: OJO Images/SuperStock; p11 top right: iStockphoto.com/ © Alexander Chernyakov; p11 bottom left: © Bogdan Hoda | Dreamstime.com; p11 bottom right: iStockphoto.com/ © Ra Photography; p13 top: Getty Images/Science Photo Library; p13 background: © Emilia Ungur | Dreamstime.com; p13 bottom right: © Diegoop | Dreamstime.com; p15 top: © Jjspring | Dreamstime.com; p15 middle right: © Jacek Chabraszewski | Dreamstime.com; p15 bottom left: © Bandesz | Dreamstime.com; p15 bottom right: iStockphoto.com/ © George Clerk; p17: © Ron Chapple | Dreamstime.com; p18 top: © Scol22 | Dreamstime.com; p18 bottom: © Sgcallaway1994 | Dreamstime.com; p19 top (and Contents page): © Photographer | Dreamstime.com; p19 bottom: © Simona Dumitru | Dreamstime.com; p20: Getty Images/Age Fotostock/Javier Larrea; p21 top: Corbis/SuperStock; p21 middle: iStockphoto.com/ © David Jones; p21 bottom: © Monika Wisniewska | Dreamstime.com; p22: © Ron Chapple | Dreamstime.com; p23: © Joyfull | Dreamstime.com; Weather icons pps 16-19: iStockphoto.com/ © Thomas Amby Johansen

Contents

The Weather

The weather is different every day. Before we plan our day, we often check the weather first.

If it is cold and wet, we might stay inside and play a game.

If it is sunny, with a blue sky, we might play outside with our friends.

When we talk about the weather, what we are really talking about is the *air, sunshine, clouds, rain* and *wind.*

Seasons

Lots of places in the world have four seasons: summer, autumn, winter and spring.

Summer is often hot and sunny.
In summer people spend lots of time outside.

Autumn means that cooler weather is coming. The leaves on some of the trees turn yellow, red and brown, and begin to drop off.

SPRING

DID YOU KNOW?

When the weather is hot, the *temperature* goes up. When the weather is cold, the temperature goes down. The temperature tells you how hot or cold the air is.

Winter is often cold and rainy,
with frost and fog.
In some places it may snow.
Lots of trees lose their leaves during winter.

frost

fog

rain

snow

Spring is when the weather becomes warmer.
The leaves on the trees grow back
and the flowers come out.
Lots of baby animals are born, too.

DID YOU KNOW?

Some places have only two seasons — wet and dry.
It is hot all the year but in 'the wet' it can rain every day.

9

Sunshine

Sunshine comes from the sun — it gives us light and keeps us warm.

In summer, the *sun's rays* are at their hottest and we must cover our skin when we are outside.

1. We need to wear a hat and *suncream*.
2. We should stay in the *shade* during the hottest part of the day.

We need warm clothes in winter even when it's sunny.

In winter, sunny days are not as warm as sunny days in summer.

Without the sun, there would be no food for us to eat. This is because plants need sunshine to grow and *farm animals* need plants to eat.

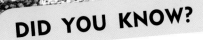

DID YOU KNOW?

While it is daytime on one side of the world, it is night-time on the other side of the world.

11

Wind

When the air around us moves,
it makes wind.
The sun warms up the ground,
and the ground warms up the air
above it.
This warm air moves up
and mixes with cool air.
When the warm air and cool air mix,
it makes wind.

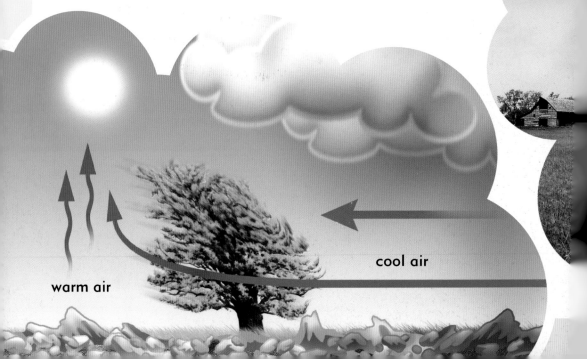

cool air

warm air

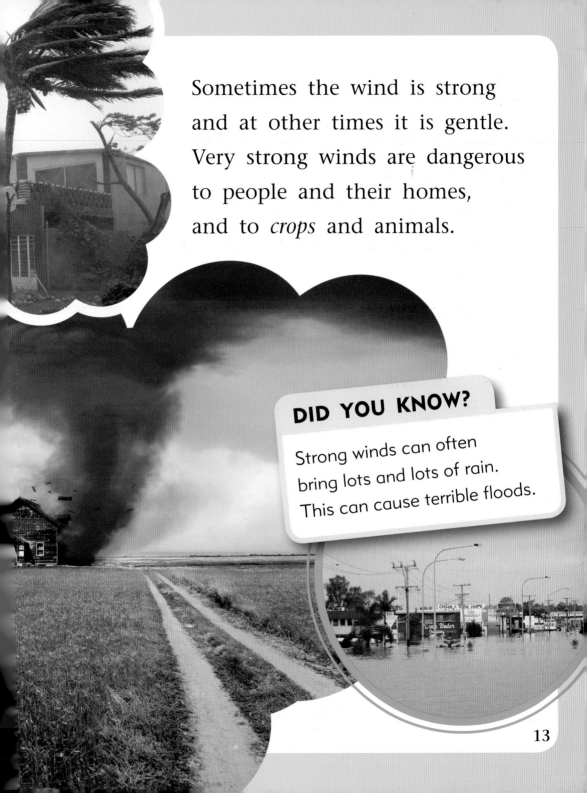

Sometimes the wind is strong and at other times it is gentle. Very strong winds are dangerous to people and their homes, and to *crops* and animals.

DID YOU KNOW?

Strong winds can often bring lots and lots of rain. This can cause terrible floods.

The Air

The air around us can be wet or dry.

The air can be wet
in cold and in hot weather.

When the air is cold and wet,
we can have snow, fog, frost, rain and hail.

SNOW

FOG

FROST

RAIN

HAIL

14

When the air is hot and wet, we can have rain and hail.

When the air is dry, there are blue skies and no rain.

When the air is wet, and mixes with wind, we can have a *storm*. There may be *thunder*, *lightning*, rain and hail.

DID YOU KNOW?

Lightning makes light patterns in the sky. It also makes a very loud noise like a rumble. We call this thunder.

Clouds

Clouds are made up of tiny drops of water, or sometimes little bits of ice.
These drops of water are so tiny and light that they float together in the air
to make a cloud.

There are many different clouds.

Thin and wispy clouds are called 'cirrus clouds'.
They are way up in the sky.
We can see these clouds
in fine, sunny weather.

FINE WEATHER

White fluffy clouds are called 'cumulus clouds'.
We can see these clouds in fine, sunny weather, too —
but sometimes they bring light rain.

Long, flat, grey clouds are called 'stratus clouds'.
These clouds often bring rain.

LIGHT RAIN

RAIN

HEAVY RAIN

Tall, dark, grey clouds
are called 'nimbus clouds'.
They can bring lightning, heavy rain,
strong wind and even a *tornado*!

DID YOU KNOW?

Fog is really a stratus cloud
down on the ground.

Watching the Weather

All over the world, the weather is being watched.

We can use *computers* and *satellites* to watch the weather.

The weather is very important
for lots of people.
People such as *pilots*, *sailors*
and *farmers* all need to find out
what the weather is going to be like.
It can be dangerous to fly, sail or work
outside if the weather is stormy or windy.

Most people check the weather every day.
It helps them to plan what they will wear
and what they will do during their day.

The weather is important to us all.
How is the weather important to your family?

Picture Glossary

air

pilots

suncream

clouds

rain

sunshine

computers

sailors

temperature

crops

satellites

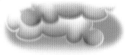

thunder

farm animals

shade

tornado

farmers

storm

wind

lightning

sun's rays